TIGERS

by Jenny Markert

Published in the United States of America by The Child's World®
1980 Lookout Drive • Mankato, MN 56003-1705
800-599-READ • www.childsworld.com

PHOTO CREDITS
© Arco Images/Alamy: 10
© blickwinkel/Alamy: 8–9
© Chris Fredriksson/Alamy: 16–17
© DLILLC/Corbis: 28
© Francois Savigny/naturepl.com: 14
© Gerard Lacz/Animals Animals–Earth Scenes: 23
© Huw Evans/Alamy: 20
© Joseph Van Os/Getty Images: 25
© Nick Garbutt/naturepl.com: 26–27
© Peter Weimann/Animals Animals–Earth Scenes: 7
© Steve Bloom Images/Alamy: cover, 1
© Theo Allofs/zefa/Corbis: 19
© Thomas Mangelsen/Minden Pictures: 5
© Thomas & Pat Leeson/Photo Researchers, Inc.: 13
© Toby Sinclair/npl/Minden Pictures: 15
© ZSSD/Minden Pictures: 27

ACKNOWLEDGMENTS
The Child's World®: Mary Berendes, Publishing Director;
Katherine Stevenson, Editor; Pamela Mitsakos, Photo Researcher;
Judy Karren, Fact Checker

The Design Lab: Kathleen Petelinsek, Design; Kari Tobin, Page Production

LIBRARY OF CONGRESS CATALOGING-IN-PUBLICATION DATA
Markert, Jenny.
 Tigers / by Jenny Markert.
 p. cm. — (New naturebooks)
 Includes index.
 ISBN-13: 978-1-59296-853-4 (library bound : alk. paper)
 ISBN-10: 1-59296-853-8 (library bound : alk. paper)
 1. Tigers—Juvenile literature. I. Title. II. Series.
 QL737.C23M27 2007
 599.756—dc22   2007000176

Table of Contents

On the cover: This Siberian tiger is enjoying a sunny day.

Meet the Tiger!

People have had many names for tigers—including "hairy face," "the striped one," and "grandfather."

The earliest tigerlike cats lived over 2 million years ago.

A tiger's paw prints are called *pugmarks*.

Deep in the rain forest, night is falling. Some animals are settling down to rest. Others are coming out to eat. A small deer walks toward a stream to get a drink. It does not see another animal hiding nearby. The other animal watches the deer carefully. Without a sound, it creeps closer. Suddenly it springs and pounces, clamping its jaws around the deer's neck. In moments the deer is dead, and the hunter drags its body away. What is this quiet, powerful hunter? It's a tiger!

This Bengal tiger is watching an animal from across a clearing.

What Are Tigers?

Each tiger has its very own pattern of stripes. The stripes go all the way down to its skin. If you shaved a tiger, its skin would show its striped pattern!

White tigers have white fur with brown stripes. They're not a different kind of tiger, they're just a different color. They're popular in zoos.

Tigers are big, wild cats. In fact, they are the biggest wild cats on Earth. These hunters are best known for their bold stripes. Most of them are orange-gold with black stripes. Their stomachs and throats are white or cream. Male tigers have slightly longer fur, called a *ruff*, around their necks. They're also bigger than the females.

Like all cats, tigers belong to a group of animals called **mammals**. Mammals have hair and warm bodies. They also feed their babies milk from their bodies. Dogs, whales, and people are mammals, too.

This Siberian tiger is cooling off on a hot day.

Are There Different Kinds of Tigers?

The Siberian tiger's thick, long coat makes it look even bigger than it is. The fur is warm enough to protect the tiger from the freezing cold of Siberia.

Recently, scientists decided that Malayan tigers from the country of Malaysia are actually a ninth subspecies.

All tigers today belong to the same **species**. Within the tiger species, there used to be eight different kinds, or *subspecies*. Three of these subspecies died out, or went **extinct**, within the last 70 years. That left only five.

Two of the remaining subspecies are the best known. The biggest are Siberian tigers, which come from Siberia, China, and North Korea. Males often grow to 10 feet (3 m) long and weigh up to 675 pounds (306 kg)! Siberian tigers have thick, light yellow coats and fewer stripes than other tigers. Bengal tigers are almost as big as Siberian tigers. They have light yellow to reddish yellow fur and come from India and nearby countries. About four-fifths of the tigers living today are Bengal tigers.

You can see how this white Bengal tiger differs from the Bengal tiger on page 14.

Three other subspecies of tigers aren't as well known to most people. Indonesian tigers come from Southeast Asia. They're a little smaller than Bengal tigers and are also darker in color. South China tigers come from central and southern China. They're smaller and have almost gone extinct. China has passed laws against killing these tigers, but it might be too late. There are only 59 known to be alive in China. Nobody has seen one in the wild for 20 years. Sumatran tigers are the smallest subspecies. A big male might weigh about 300 pounds (136 kg). These tigers come from the thick forests on the island of Sumatra, in Indonesia.

Tigers have good eyesight and can see well at night, but they rely even more on their keen hearing.

Tigers don't roar as often as lions do. Tigers roar when they want to find a mate or scare another tiger away.

You can easily hear a tiger's roar from 2 miles (3 km) away!

This Sumatran tiger is watching some birds from across a field.

Where Do Tigers Live?

Many kinds of cats don't like water. But tigers love it! In hot weather, they swim to cool off. They often enter the water backwards, probably to keep it out of their eyes.

Sometimes tigers even catch and kill animals while swimming.

A tiger's claws can be up to 5 inches (almost 13 cm) long!

Today, wild tigers live only in scattered parts of Asia, from Siberia to India and Southeast Asia. They used to live in many more parts of Asia. But people have taken over most of these areas and left few places for the tigers to live.

Tigers live in many different **habitats**— especially forests, but also grasslands and swamps. In the south, their living places are often warm, moist rain forests. Farther north, some even live in cold, snowy mountains. Overall, tigers do best in places with lots of plants in which to hide. There the tiger's stripes and colors act as **camouflage**. They help the tiger blend in with grasses and shadows. Tigers also need a good supply of their favorite food animals and a good supply of water.

Siberian tigers are used to snowy surroundings. They live in colder areas of Siberia, China, and North Korea. These cats are also called Amur tigers.

These scratch marks were left by a Bengal tiger in India's Kaziranga National Park.

Most tigers live and hunt by themselves. A single tiger lives, hunts, and sleeps in a home range of its own. A male's home range might overlap the ranges of several females. But the male does not let other males enter its **territory**. In fact, males often fight over their territories—sometimes to the death.

To avoid fighting, male tigers mark the edges of their territories. They leave smells, body waste, and scrape marks to tell other males, "Keep out!" Tigers use their sense of smell to learn all about their neighbors. They know how many tigers live in the area. They know whether they are males or females, and whether they are from the area or are strangers.

Tigers make lots of different sounds to communicate with other tigers. When they growl or snarl, it means to stay away. Like housecats, they use tail movements to communicate, too.

Tigers can run as fast as 37 miles (60 km) an hour, for short distances.

Tigers can jump as high as 16 feet (5 m) and as far as 30 feet (9 m).

Here you can see a male Bengal tiger scratching a tree in India.

What Do Tigers Eat?

Even hunting alone, tigers can catch and kill animals much bigger than themselves.

Tigers prefer to catch bigger animals because they provide enough meat for several days.

Tigers can climb trees very well, although they don't do it often.

Tigers are meat-eating **predators** that hunt other animals for food. The animals they eat are called their **prey**. Tigers that live in different places eat different kinds of prey. Their favorite foods are medium-sized or bigger plant-eaters, such as deer, antelope, young wild pigs, and water buffalo. But they eat other kinds of animals, too, including fish and birds. Sometimes they even eat other predators, such as bears and leopards! And sometimes they kill young elephants or rhinos that are not well protected by their herds. If they happen to find dead animals, they will eat those, too.

You can see how this Bengal tiger pulls on the meat as it feeds.

How Do Tigers Hunt?

Tigers have soft pads on the bottoms of their feet. The pads help the tigers move silently and surprise their prey.

Even for tigers, hunting isn't easy. Out of 20 attacks, they might end up with dinner in only one or two.

When a tiger is chasing prey, its long tail helps it keep its balance as it turns.

Tigers start hunting just after sundown. They hunt by **ambush**, which means that they hide and surprise their prey. Often they search for prey near water holes, where they know animals will come to drink. When an animal finally comes close, the tiger creeps toward it, crouching low. Suddenly, it leaps out and runs after its surprised prey. When it catches up, it uses its powerful front paws to knock the animal down. Then it uses its big teeth to bite the animal's neck.

18

This Bengal tiger is stalking prey in India's Bandhavgarh National Park.

If a tiger kills an animal out in the open, it drags its meal to a safer place. Once the tiger finds a quiet spot, it eats until it's full. A tiger can eat 65 pounds (29 kg) or more of meat at a time. That would be like you eating 300 hot dogs for dinner!

After the tiger eats, its belly is full. And after working so hard, the tiger is ready to take a long nap. Before it goes to sleep, the tiger hides any meat it didn't eat. It covers these leftovers with grass, leaves, or tree branches. When the tiger wakes up and feels hungry again, it uncovers its dinner and eats some more.

To stay alive, an adult tiger must catch about 7,000 pounds (3,175 kg) of prey in a year.

Tigers are strong enough to drag dead animals that weigh twice as much as they do.

Tigers have 30 teeth. Some of them help the tiger bite and hold onto its prey. Others are good for tearing, slicing, and chewing meat.

You can see how this Siberian tiger uses its big teeth to tear at its meal.

21

What Are Baby Tigers Like?

At first, tiger cubs spend most of their time in their den. The mother leaves them there while she hunts, and brings them their dinner. But she keeps the den clean and doesn't bring the meat inside.

Half of all tiger cubs die in their first two years. Many are killed by people or by predators such as hyenas, jackals, wild dogs, and pythons.

Baby tigers are called *cubs*. A mother tiger usually has two to four cubs in a **litter**. When tiger cubs are very small, all they drink is their mother's milk. As they grow bigger, they begin to eat meat their mother brings them. The cubs stay with their mother for their first two years. With only one adult to care for them, they are often in danger. The mother protects them and teaches them how to hunt. When they can hunt well enough, the young tigers leave their mother. They search for their own places to live. Young females often live near their mother. Young males must fight other males to take over a territory.

This Bengal tiger cub is only eight weeks old.

Are Tigers Dangerous?

A single blow from a tiger's paw can kill a human.

Only three out of a thousand tigers will end up attacking people.

Snakebites kill a hundred times more people than tigers do.

Tigers are big, strong, and fast. With their pointed teeth and sharp claws, they can be very dangerous! Many people think that tigers like to hunt and eat people. That isn't true. Usually they are afraid of people. It is rare for tigers to attack them instead. Sometimes tigers attack people if they feel surprised or threatened. Sometimes they attack because they cannot catch other prey— usually because they are old, hurt, or missing too many teeth. These "man-eating" tigers are usually caught and killed.

When threatened, tigers show their teeth and make hissing noises. This warns attackers to stay away! If an attacker keeps coming, the tiger swats with its strong front legs, or pounces on the enemy.

Are Tigers in Danger?

A hundred years ago, there were probably 100,000 wild tigers. By the 1970s, there were only 4,000.

Some people make lots of money by hunting tigers illegally, either killing the tigers or catching them to sell. A single tiger can bring up to $50,000. Hunting animals illegally is called *poaching*.

Baby tigers are always in danger of being eaten by other animals. Lions, crocodiles, and wild dogs steal tiger cubs from their mothers. Sometimes, if they are really hungry, other tigers will even eat cubs.

Adult tigers are in little danger from other animals. But they are in a great deal of danger from people. People have hunted tigers for sport and for their brightly striped skins. In some places, people kill tigers to use their body parts in medicines. Tiger body parts have never been proved to cure illnesses, but some people believe that they do. Cutting down forests, farming, and building roads, dams, and towns have also destroyed many of the tigers' habitats.

Sumatran tigers like this one are becoming very rare. This one lives in a zoo.

Today, tigers are said to be **endangered**. Nobody knows exactly how many are left in the world. Most tigers today live in zoos or parks. There are probably only 5,000 to 7,000 left in the wild. Scientists are worried about whether wild tigers can still be saved. Many countries have passed laws to keep people from killing tigers or using their body parts in medicines. Even so, poaching is still a big problem. But some people and governments are working to save places where the tigers can live. And scientists are studying these colorful animals to learn all they can. Many people still hope to find ways to keep these amazing animals living free.

In the wild, tigers can live to be 12 to 15 years old. In zoos or parks, they can live to be 20 or more.

Today, the country with the largest number of tigers is the United States! Some 12,000 tigers live there—although not in the wild.

From far away, this Bengal tiger would be hard to see. Its stripes would help it to blend in with the nearby leaves.

29

Glossary

ambush (AM-bush) In an ambush, an attacker hides and then takes someone by surprise. Tigers hunt by ambush.

camouflage (KA-muh-flazh) Camouflage is special coloring or markings that help an animal blend in with its surroundings. Tigers' stripes act as camouflage.

endangered (in-DAYN-jurd) An endangered animal is one that is close to dying out completely. Tigers are endangered.

extinct (ek-STINKT) An extinct animal or plant is one that has completely died out. Some kinds of tigers are now extinct.

habitats (HA-bih-tats) Animals' habitats are the types of surroundings in which the animals live. Tigers live in a wide range of habitats.

litter (LIH-tur) A litter is a group of babies born to one animal at the same time. Tigers usually have two to four cubs in a litter.

mammals (MAM-ullz) Mammals are warm-blooded animals that have hair on their bodies and feed their babies milk from the mother's body. Tigers are mammals.

predators (PREH-duh-terz) Predators are animals that hunt and kill other animals for food. Tigers are predators.

prey (PRAY) Prey are animals that other animals hunt as food. Tigers can kill prey much larger than themselves.

species (SPEE-sheez) An animal species is a group of animals that share the same features and have babies with animals in the same group. All tigers belong to the same species.

territory (TEHR-uh-tor-ee) An animal's territory is the area that the animal claims as its own and defends against outsiders. A male tiger fights to keep other male tigers out of his territory.

To Find Out More

Watch It!

Discovery Channel. *Living with Tigers*. DVD. Discovery Communications, 2004.

National Geographic Society. *Hidden World of the Bengal Tiger*. VHS. Washington, D.C.: National Geographic Video, 1999.

National Geographic Society. *Tigers of the Snow*. DVD. Washington, D.C. : National Geographic Video, 1996.

Read It!

DuTemple, Lesley A. *Tigers*. Minneapolis, MN: Lerner Publications, 1996.

Seidensticker, John. *Tigers*. Stillwater, MN: Voyageur Press, 1996.

Squire, Ann. *Tigers*. New York: Children's Press, 2005.

Thomson, Sarah L. *Tigers*. New York: HarperCollins, 2004.

On the Web

Visit our Web page for lots of links about tigers:
http://www.childsworld.com/links

Note to Parents, Teachers, and Librarians: We routinely check our Web links to make sure they're safe, active sites—so encourage your readers to check them out!

Index